Sleeping in an Empty Room

Omave Mance

close your eyes and breathe

DEDICATION

For all those who believed

CONTENTS

	Acknowledgments	i
1	Alzheimer's Diary	1
2	Where I'm From	Pg 3
3	Sleeping in an Empty Room	Pg 7
4	Lime and Smile	Pg 9
5	Ride and Armstrong	Pg 10
6	The Dark Ones	Pg 13
7	REDactED 910pm	Pg 14
8	Reburn	Pg 16
9	Men are such Dogs	Pg 17
10	For the Birds	Pg 18

ACKNOWLEDGMENTS

This is not an objective truth.
This is somewhere between gospel and confession.
I acknowledge that it might not be safe.

I know that

and I must.

ALZHEIMER'''S DIARY

Memory is a funny thing;
the way it knots and molds,
unravels, and falls away.

You resurrected
An obsession
I thought was cleanly
massaged from my brain.

It's funny how
a story or a smile
can be a spell,
that calls back the dead
or dying.

The way I remember
the scent on your neck
and you remember
romance.

We both call back

SLEEPING IN AN EMPTYY ROOM

an incomplete corpse,

and make it dance;
untangle itself
and we twist it
till it falls away.

I always thought I'd forget you;

Just not this way.

WHERE I'M FROM

I'm from the front lines
of a class war.

Where girls,
gifted nose jobs for sweet sixteen,
piss and cheat off girls who
take extra tampons home
from the school nurse.

I'm from slap-box
and soapbox
and permanent record.

From your classmates'
Dad's yacht and Costco pizza.

I'm from where
"Teach me how to Dougie "
and "Bohemian Rhapsody"
are both threats.

SLEEPING IN AN EMPTYY ROOM

I'm from empty pools
and essays;
written on metro windows.

I'm from bottled water
preferences and toilet water
syringes.

I'm from vintage shopping
Afterschool and Swap Meet
weekends.

From church flannel
and church shoes.

I'm from garden hose
summers and
Garden Party language.

From over the hill
and back before late.

From "My moms super chill"
and "My dads away on business"

from "That frozen chicken better not be in there with them
dirty dishes".

I'm from
too many cleared chambers
and not enough clear memories.

SLEEPING IN AN EMPTYY ROOM

I'm from prayer warriors
and halfway pimps.

From the soil and the pit

and the compost next to the
plastics bin
outside the on-campus
military recruiting
office.

I'm from white homies
and black colleges
and "What's her name got into
'The Movies'
because her brother OD'ed last summer.

I'm from wave cap
from shop owners with straight hair
and shop owners that don't
wave back
straight face they just
hold their hands below the counter
and stare.

I'm from
house party
and day party
and warehouse party
and trash and bash

but always vote
The Republican Party

I'm from the 818

and 323 and 310
and 213

I'm from the 750
to the 761 the
405 to the 101

Triple digit summers
and single digits friends

I'm from where
if you want to see
the water

You don't have to
take the 10.

SLEEPING IN AN EMPTY ROOM

I haven't had a full night's sleep
for longer than I can remember.

The water calls me
like a desperate lover-

choker and pouty eyes.

Then, the porcelain
begs me to fill the void.

The glowing screen
steals me from sleep
and
I run away with her-

short skirt and long eyelashes.

To the world I am sleeping.

To the girl-
I'm still sleeping.

SLEEPING IN AN EMPTYY ROOM

The only peace is in these hours.

The only real release is strained and sour.

Best rest I've had in weeks

was slumped like a junkie

hugged whole

by a cool tile
and a warm shower.

LIME AND SMILE

Is it still temptation
when its' still on my lips-
bitter and sweet-
twice in one long,
long week?

Is it temporary
when the salt and heat
are more than just a memory?

Is it fever?

Is it stepped on?

Is it in?
Is it safe?
Is it real?

Is it real?

Is it….

Still temptation?

RIDE AND ARMSTRONG

We walked
for what seemed like
all afternoon
to the top of the hill

where we come
just to
see how far
we've come

We walked
at a snail's pace

Hand in hand

Handling the gravity
like a hot stone

We walked
on light beams
like the dark was lava-
bounced down toward the home
we had always imagined

I knew if you fell
or I stumbled
there was no
easy way back.

We tried a kiss
and only the leaves
and moonbeams
and tracks

We left-
could watch us
miss

We existed
outside

space
and time
was ours

We were
comfortable.

We knew
not to call it love
like the word was
a hex

But the feeling
of being seen

having partner
and witness
was a blessing

So, we kept walking
and that was enough.

That was enough for us.

THE DARK ONES

When we're texting;
it feels like speed chess
in the loneliest park.

I hit send
and sigh relief,

and smile with the deepest
parts of me.

REDACTED 910PM

I am living my private life
as if someone is watching.
I am entertaining a theory
that God has A.D.D.
and I must keep it
so interesting that my eyes combust
or face eternal damnation.

I haven't kept a journal since I was old enough to know better.

This is a poor excuse for a diary.
I am not good at believing in safety anymore.

I hold on to my true secrets.
They are heirlooms given to me by my purest self.
I pray I am never so far gone
that I feel the need to have them appraised.

I pray if I am blessed with children
that they don't lament how they were raised.

I am terribly disappointed in the way I take care of my body.

I am terrified that I will treat my children the same.

I don't think I'm afraid that I'm ungodly.
I   think   I'm   afraid   God   made   me   this   way.

REBURN

The sin
is never the blissful climax
we've been told to fear.

It's a dull punch-
a numbered blade that bares your name
and
an awkward hotel check in.

Like the teacher's lounge
or your midnight closet;
the fantasy
never quite beats
imagination.

MEN ARE SUCH DOGS

I understand the dogs
chasing cars,
trying to remember the wind.

Tongue out the window
like a white flag,
surrendered to the bliss.

It always ends with
You.

Your eyes,
and laugh
and fingertips.

FOR THE BIRDS

It always ends with birds.

Stork
plucked you from the clouds.

                                            Vulture
                    making last meal of your carcass.

                        Pigeon
        steals your food and humbles you
            with a well-placed shit.

Dove
gives you hope
or some white washed fairytale.

                                              Crow
                  remembers you are mortal
                            and laughs.

Owl
rules the nights and sees everything.

            It always ends with the birds.

The Geese
warn of winter

                                          and Rooster
                                         calls for the sun.

The Gulls
lead you to water

                and the Sparrow
                  sings for God.

                I have forgotten
            where to aim my voice;

            when God is on the ground.

ABOUT THE AUTHOR

Read the work and mind your business.

www.ingramcontent.com/pod-product-compliance
Lightning Source LLC
Chambersburg PA
CBHW032311240526
45464CB00023BA/2986